HARVEST OF RIGHTEOUSNESS

HARVEST OF RIGHTEOUSNESS

A Spiritual Discipline of Devotion in the Reformed Tradition

REBECCA BRADBURN LANGER

Geneva Press
Louisville, Kentucky

Scripture quotations, unless otherwise noted, are from the New Revised Standard Version of the Bible, copyright © 1989 by the Division of Christian Education of the National Council of the Churches of Christ in the U.S.A., and are used by permission.

Some scripture verses are from *An Inclusive Language Lectionary, Readings for Year B,* copyright 1987 by the Division of Education and Ministry, National Council of the Churches of Christ in the U.S.A. Used by permission. All rights reserved. Lectionary texts are based on the Revised Standard Version of the Bible, copyright 1946, 1952, and 1971 by the Division of Christian Education of the National Council of the Churches of Christ in the U.S.A.

Passages have been excerpted from *With Open Hands* by Henri J. M. Nouwen. Copyright 1995 by Ave Maria Press, Notre Dame, IN 46556. Used with permission of the publisher.

Howard Thurman quotes from Anne Thurman's *For the Inward Journey: The Writings of Howard Thurman* (Richmond, Ind.: Friends United Press, 1991) are used by permission of Friends United Press.

Book design by Douglas & Gayle Ltd. and Carol Johnson
Cover design by Kevin Darst
Cover illustration by Rebecca Langer

First edition
Published by Westminster John Knox Press
Louisville, Kentucky

This book is printed on acid-free paper that meets the American National Standards Institute Z39.48 standard. ⊗

PRINTED IN THE UNITED STATES OF AMERICA
99 00 01 02 03 04 05 06 07 08 — 10 9 8 7 6 5 4 3 2

Library of Congress Cataloging-in-Publication Data

Langer, Rebecca Bradburn.
    Harvest of righteousness : a spiritual discipline of devotion in the Reformed tradition / Rebecca Bradburn Langer. — 1st ed.
        p.   cm.
    ISBN 0-664-50028-5 (alk. paper)
    1. Devotional exercises.   2. Spiritual life—Presbyterian Church.
3. Presbyterian Church—Prayer-books and devotions—English.
I. Title
BX9187.L36   1998
248.4'6—dc21
                                                    98-18699

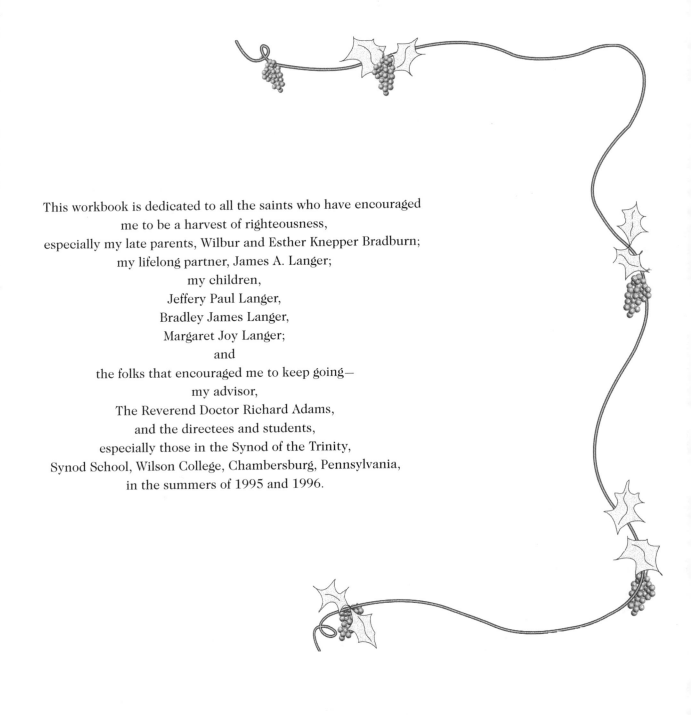

This workbook is dedicated to all the saints who have encouraged
me to be a harvest of righteousness,
especially my late parents, Wilbur and Esther Knepper Bradburn;
my lifelong partner, James A. Langer;
my children,
Jeffery Paul Langer,
Bradley James Langer,
Margaret Joy Langer;
and
the folks that encouraged me to keep going—
my advisor,
The Reverend Doctor Richard Adams,
and the directees and students,
especially those in the Synod of the Trinity,
Synod School, Wilson College, Chambersburg, Pennsylvania,
in the summers of 1995 and 1996.

Harvest of Righteousness

Hymn to the tune of Crimond
(*Presbyterian Hymnal* 170)

Along the journey there will be
Some good and surely ill,
But God is with us all the way
And journeys with us still.

God plants the seeds of right within
And nurtures as they grow,
Turn to the light of God's desire
And righteous we will grow.

So in our lives forever be
Returning to our God,
Reflecting all the Savior taught
And growing in God's love.

A harvest of God's righteousness
Most surely is our call,
Justice and mercy bursting forth
To praise the All in All.

—Rebecca Bradburn Langer, 1995

Introduction

This workbook presents a four-week exploration of spiritual disciplines, designed especially, but not exclusively, for Presbyterians and others in the Reformed theological tradition. The title *Harvest of Righteousness* comes from the picture of spiritual growth found in Philippians 1:9–11: "And this is my prayer, that your love may overflow more and more with knowledge and full insight to help you to determine what is best, so that in the day of Christ you may be pure and blameless, having produced the harvest of righteousness that comes through Jesus Christ for the glory and praise of God."

As we grow in God, each of us becomes a "harvest of righteousness." Beginning like a tiny seed, our lives of faith can grow to full stature. This growth occurs through God's grace, not because of our practices of devotion in the spiritual disciplines but because spiritual disciplines are a means, a way of opening to God. The practice of the disciplines is one way we respond with thanksgiving and gratefulness to God's love for us. One of the purposes of this workbook is for the participants, by the end of the four weeks, to have a clearer sense of ways to give thanks to God in their daily personal worship.

The goal of the workbook is to establish a daily routine of personal worship using the spiritual disciplines. By spiritual disciplines we mean intentional acts of devotion for the purpose of seeking God's direction in one's life. Authors differ as to the exact activities that constitute spiritual disciplines, but included in the list can be such things as worship, service, prayer, fasting, practicing solitude, giving of time and talent, and reading and reflecting on scripture. In the Old Testament, the command to "do justice, and to love kindness, and to walk humbly with your God" (Micah 6:8) is a call to spiritual discipline. In Matthew 6, Jesus teaches the disciplines of praying, fasting, and giving. Indeed, the Bible provides primary guidance for people of the Reformed tradition concerning spiritual disciplines, and, therefore, this workbook will emphasize use of the Bible as the primary resource for the practice of spiritual disciplines—employing a method of devotional reading.

We are all to reflect the image of God indelibly stamped on our souls. This is a lifelong task that happens as the seeds of God's grace are nourished in our lives. The workbook is an invitation to practice spiritual disciplines as a way of opening one's life to God's Word. The spiritual disciplines are the soil and sustenance for the seeds of grace in our lives. Of these disciplines, Howard Rice says, "Our use of means of grace is not for the purpose of satisfying God, but for the renewal of our lives" (Rice 1991, 197).

The purpose, then, of practicing the spiritual disciplines is to become more and more like Jesus, the Righteous One (Acts 7:52). Simply working through these exercises will not make one grow into holiness. The purpose of the workbook is not to set up practices that somehow earn God's favor, for we are already favored in God's sight, as Paul tells us in Romans, "Once you were no people, but now you are God's people" (1 Peter 2:10, RSV). Despite our sinfulness, God has created us good and called us God's own.

Reformed Christians have emphasized the discipline of corporate and personal worship. In the *Directions of the General Assembly* (1647), personal worship is called "secret worship." Spiritual disciplines have been practiced by God's covenant people from Old Testament times forward. John Calvin describes this process:

> And, indeed, this restoration does not take place in one moment or one day or one year; but through continual and sometimes even slow advances God wipes out in his elect the corruptions of the flesh, cleanses them of guilt, consecrates them to himself as temples, renewing all their minds to true purity that they may practice repentance throughout their lives and know that this warfare will end only in death.
>
> (Calvin 1960, III/3/9)

Using the Workbook

The workbook is designed to aid individuals and small groups in the practice of daily personal worship. The tremendous rush of life today often erodes faithful practice of the disciplines, and it is difficult to maintain a balanced life. This workbook will encourage the practice of worshiping every day. But our individual worship should lead us toward worship with others. Daily personal worship is the seedbed for the weekly group worship. The Reformed tradition has always emphasized both corporate and personal worship, but most of us find corporate worship to be an easier discipline to keep than daily personal worship. While a person can use the workbook alone, support of a small group is more helpful in seeking to pay attention to God. The group acts as the extended community of faith. This is consistent with the Reformed tradition's insistence on discerning God's Word in a context larger than one's own thoughts and feelings. The group helps discern and support God's movements in one's private and personal life.

In the four-week commitment involved in using this workbook, participants are urged to be gentle with themselves as they seek to develop and deepen their spiritual life. It takes time and practice to establish a discipline, like planting seeds in a garden. To develop a garden the seeds need patient tending. The workbook approach is a "more with less" approach. For example, during each of the four weeks, the same biblical text is read and reflected on every day of that week. Although this may seem repetitive, or even boring, the process is aimed at overcoming our tendency to race through scripture. In reading the Bible, the goal is not speed-reading but a slow, relaxed process, one that Marjorie Thompson refers to in *Soul Feast* as something like chewing a cud: "It is a matter of taking in the bread of God's Word, chewing on it, and digesting it until it brings forth new life and energy that can be shared with others" (Thompson 1995, 25). Unfortunately, we are used to a "fast-food" mentality, which causes us to dash from one thing in the Bible to another without receiving the full nourishment of each passage. Devotional reading of scripture will prove to be deeply satisfying if one can gently keep with it.

Since the disciplines can be "spiritual watering" for our souls, there is a balance of activities in the workbook for body, mind, and spirit. These activities are to encourage listening to the scripture in a variety of ways, using both head-learnings and heart-learnings. In the Reformed tradition, mind (or head) activity has often been the most emphasized. The workbook issues an invitation to integrate body, mind, and spirit through artwork, physical motion, and other resources and activities.

In an effort to bring balance to the workbook, some writings by women have been added that do not necessarily come from the Reformed tradition. In one sense, this drawing on others grows out of the openness with which the Reformed tradition has embraced other Christian traditions.

It is important to see how the format of this workbook matches categories of personal worship to corresponding categories in corporate worship. The workbook's daily rhythm and corporate worship (usually on the Lord's Day) have a similar pattern, namely (1) Rest, (2) Read and Reflect, (3) Pray, and (4) Respond:

1. Preparing for the Word—Resting

The rhythm of daily worship begins by preparing for the Word, what we are calling "resting." The purpose of resting is to "be still and know God" (Psalm 46:10). This private resting corresponds to the preparation, the "resting," of corporate worship, which often takes the form of a musical prelude. (In private worship music can also be used. Try, for example, some of the music tapes from the Taize community ["Songs of Prayer" or "Sing to God" from GIA Publications, Inc.].) Silence is another way to help one become more centered and ready to listen for God. Also, visual art can be used as a focus point to settle oneself to rest in God. To do this, find, in a book or elsewhere, an appealing work of art and let yourself "rest" in the color or movement.

Repetition of the suggested prayer for beginning each day may also be helpful as one settles in to listen for God.

2. Hearing the Word—Reading and Reflecting through Devotional Reading

Just as corporate worship involves the reading of scripture, so each of the weeks in this four-week program of daily worship has a main scripture passage for devotional reading. This main scripture is read every day of that week (more scriptures and materials for reflection each week can be found in the pages called "Additional Reflection Selections"). In the devotional practice of the Reformed tradition, the Bible reading is often done in the manner called *lectio divina*. This method of devotional reading is a way of listening for a word or phrase that seems to "call" to the reader. The Reformed tradition has stood firm in the belief of the power of God's Word as a foundation for life and a guide for spiritual maturation. While much of the Reformed tradition has emphasized the more scholarly approach to the Word, devotional reading was encouraged by Calvin as a way of listening for God. There is a vital role, of course, for careful scholarship in working with scripture, but there is also a need for individuals to listen for the Word of God with different ears. The purpose of devotional reading is to engage scripture so that one's relationship with God is strengthened and to find guidance and clarity to live out one's baptismal call in the world. The process of listening for the sacred Word will be the core way of reading and reflecting on the scripture. What is offered in devotional reading differs from the study of scripture and has as its purpose reflecting on the Word for personal guidance and strength.

3. Praying in Corporate Worship— Praying in Personal Prayer

The *Book of Order* of the Presbyterian Church (U.S.A.)

defines prayer as "a conscious opening of the self to God, who initiates communion and communication with us. Prayer is receiving and responding, speaking and listening, waiting and acting in the presence of God" (W-5.40002). Prayer is developing a relationship with God where one can be fully open and honest. Calvin speaks of knowledge of self and knowledge of God. Prayer is a time of listening for God's movements in your heart and mind. Often prayer is in worded form, but it could also be some form of creative expression. In each day's exercises, the prayer time following the devotional reading could be offered while taking a walk or drawing a picture. It may also mean quiet prayer without words. One of the keys to personal worship is finding the way that you pray most naturally. Prayer in personal devotional time includes the needs of the one praying, especially in relationship to the word or phrase from scripture, as well as the needs of the church, the world, and others. Julian of Norwich said, "The fruit and the purpose of prayer is to be oned with and like God in all things" (Doyle 1983, 70). Scripture and prayer are linked and crucial to "growing" in the harvest of righteousness.

4. Responding to the Word—Responding in Personal Worship

In the flow of Rest, Read and Reflect, Pray, and Respond, the last movement is to respond appropriately to God's message. This response is the resulting fruit of the time spent reading, reflecting, and praying to God. Response is the natural outgrowth of spending time in personal worship, and the response may be a specific act or simply a deepening silence. The key is to be open to God's guidance through the use of your heart and mind and body. Response is purposeful movement in the direction one feels God nudging in the personal worship time. It may be repentance over something that has been raised in the personal devotion time or a response of writing a letter or visiting a person, or perhaps just being still, quietly enjoying the gift God has given in the time.

Righteousness has the connotation of not only doing right but, more important, doing justice (see Micah 6:8; Hosea 10:12). Much of present-day understanding of "righteousness" is bereft of justice, but the Reformed tradition has always encouraged an active spirituality, a spirituality that manifests itself by following the risen Christ into the struggles of the world. Consequently, response may mean not only involvement in applying God's word to one's personal life but engaging the world in the struggle for rights for all humankind, holding in tension the journey inward in prayer and reflection and the journey outward in response to God's Word.

Personal Expression in Encountering the Word

Another important aspect of using the workbook is for you to experiment with the variety of ways that God's Word speaks to you. Each of us is unique. God opens the path on our journeys in ways fitted to our individual needs. Do what you feel God is leading you to do in the biblical passage. Expressing what the Word means may not necessarily take the form of words. It may, for example, be expressed in an image. When reading a biblical passage, one may be led to draw or do a physical movement to express feelings or thoughts gleaned from the passage. Write a poem or a prayer that expresses what speaks to you from the passage. Experiment. Look for new ways to be open to God. Trust your instincts and work against old biases that make you feel you cannot or should not worship God in such a way. Use the workbook pages to record your experiences with scripture or keep a separate journal or sketchbook.

Created as unique individuals, each of us will experience the written Word in different ways. Every week, on the seventh day, you will meet with your group to listen to the same scripture you have been reading through the week and to celebrate how God is at work in you and your fellow journeyers. It is important that you do the workbook daily rather than leave it to the last minute. The idea is to begin to notice God each and every day.

Guidelines for Groups

If you are going to meet in a church, get permission from the church officers. Before the group comes together the first time, distribute the workbooks and ask all persons in the group to read the Introduction, so they can have an idea of what kind of commitment is involved. When the group gets together for its first meeting, it should choose a specific day each week to meet and should also select a facilitator, whose job it is to help the group follow the process (this facilitator can be the same each week, or people could take turns leading the group).

The small group should be

—No larger than 8–10 people

—Committed to a daily devotional time of 30–60 minutes

—Committed to an initial meeting and four weekly meetings with the group (this means being present except in the case of an emergency)

—Committed to a balance of silence and response time ("I pass" is always an appropriate response in the group)

—Committed to a covenant of confidentiality regarding information shared

Suggestion: Plant some seeds at the beginning class and watch them develop as the weeks progress. Sunflower seeds are a good choice or paper white bulbs.

Initial Group Meeting

1. Begin with the group sitting in a circle, and start with a few minutes of silence. A silent time helps people settle down and rest in the presence of each other and God. A simple prayer might be offered, such as the following:

Spirit of the living God, surround us in this time and in this study together. Lead us as you have led your followers since the beginning of time. May we hear your Word and bear witness to it by the fruits of our lives. Amen.

Read Galatians 5:22–26 and ask all participants to listen for the word or phrase that "jumps" out to them.

2. Introduce each other by naming a "fruit" you believe God is producing in your life—or a fruit you would like to be producing.

3. Review the guidelines for groups and also the daily instructions for devotional reading on page 10.

4. Take time for group members to discuss any questions they have about the next four weeks. It may be helpful to pick prayer partners in the group. Each partner will intentionally pray for the needs and well-being of the other person as the group proceeds.

5. Close in prayer by having each person write on a 3- x 5-inch card the desire he or she has for the remaining four weeks and read that as a prayer request, closing with the Lord's Prayer. Begin the next day with Week One—Day One of the workbook.

It may be helpful to keep some medium of art, a journal, and a Bible close as you use the workbook. A set time for daily devotions will help in keeping the daily discipline.

Prayer Partner's Name:

How to Do Devotional Reading

Each day of the week follow the outline of

Rest,

Read and Reflect,

Pray,

and Respond.

1) Rest. Be still and invite God to open your heart and mind to understanding.

2) Read devotionally . . . .

3) Pray for insight as to why this word or phrase may be important to you and what God would have you understand from it. Pray for understanding and the ability to respond as a living sacrifice, today.

4) Respond. To what are you called by your time in reflection and prayer?

cut out bookmark along dotted lines

How to Do Devotional Reading

Each day of the week follow the outline of Rest, Read and Reflect, Pray, and Respond. Use the devotional reading process below when you read the scripture. You can record your insights, thoughts, and struggles in the workbook or in a separate journal.

1) Rest. Be still and invite God to open your heart and mind to understanding.

2) Read devotionally:

—Read the scripture aloud, then pause.

—Read the scripture a second time, listening for the word or phrase that jumps out to you, the one that seems to "resonate" with you.

—Repeat that word or phrase quietly over and over, perhaps 5–10 times or more.

—Write the word or phrase on the workbook page, resting in the word.

—Draw a picture of the image that comes with this word, or write the feelings aroused by the word or phrase. You may want to respond to this in a way that seems most appropriate for you—a picture, poem, a movement, and so forth.

—Ask yourself, "What is it that God may want me to hear from this word?"

3) Pray for insight as to why this word or phrase may be important to you and what God would have you understand from it. Pray for understanding and the ability to respond as a living sacrifice, today.

4) Respond. To what are you called by your time in reflection and prayer?

Daily Reflections

Week One

Day One

REST*

Lord, open unto me
 Open unto me—light for my darkness.
 Open unto me—courage for my fear.
 Open unto me—hope for my despair.
 Open unto me—peace for my turmoil.
 Open unto me—joy for my sorrow.
 Open unto me—strength for my weakness.
 Open unto me—wisdom for my confusion.
 Open unto me—forgiveness for my sin.
 Open unto me—love for my hates.
 Open unto me—thy Self for my self.
Lord, Lord, open unto me!

Howard Thurman

*Option: Use favorite art or Taize music for resting.

READ DEVOTIONALLY

(For devotional reading process, see page 10.)

⁶The point is this: the one who sows sparingly will also reap sparingly, and the one who sows bountifully will also reap bountifully. ⁷Each of you must give as you have made up your mind, not reluctantly or under compulsion, for God loves a cheerful giver. ⁸And God is able to provide you with every blessing in abundance, so that by always having enough of everything, you may share abundantly in every good work. ⁹As it is written, "He scatters abroad, he gives to the poor; his righteousness endures forever." ¹⁰He who

supplies seed to the sower and bread for food will supply and multiply your seed for sowing and increase the harvest of your righteousness. [11]You will be enriched in every way for your great generosity, which will produce thanksgiving to God through us; [12]for the rendering of this ministry not only supplies the needs of the saints but also overflows with many thanksgivings to God. [13]Through the testing of this ministry you glorify God by your obedience to the confession of the gospel of Christ and by the generosity of your sharing with them and with all others, [14]while they long for you and pray for you because of the surpassing grace of God that he has given you. [15]Thanks be to God for his indescribable gift! *(2 Corinthians 9: 6–15)*

REFLECT

What word or phrase "speaks" to you in this passage? Record here:

Take a color that expresses what the word or phrase says to you and make a line or picture with this color. Or make a body motion that expresses the word or phrase and repeat it slowly a few times.

What are you being asked to give God? What do you need from God in order to give that gift? What gift are you "sowing" for God?

PRAY

Write or draw a prayer if you like.

RESPOND

To what response is God calling you?

Remember, you may use the additional reflection selections at the end of Week One, also.

Day Two

REST[*]

Lord, open unto me
> Open unto me—light for my darkness.
> Open unto me—courage for my fear.
> Open unto me—hope for my despair.
> Open unto me—peace for my turmoil.
> Open unto me—joy for my sorrow.
> Open unto me—strength for my weakness.
> Open unto me—wisdom for my confusion.
> Open unto me—forgiveness for my sin.
> Open unto me—love for my hates.
> Open unto me—thy Self for my self.
Lord, Lord, open unto me!

Howard Thurman

*Option: Use favorite art or Taize music for resting.

READ AND REFLECT

⁶The point is this: the one who sows sparingly will also reap sparingly, and the one who sows bountifully will also reap bountifully. ⁷Each of you must give as you have made up your mind, not reluctantly or under compulsion, for God loves a cheerful giver. ⁸And God is able to provide you with every blessing in abundance, so that by always having enough of everything, you may share abundantly in every good work. ⁹As it is written, "He scatters abroad, he gives to the poor; his righteousness endures forever." ¹⁰He who supplies seed to the sower and bread for food will supply and multiply your seed for sowing and increase the harvest of your righteousness. ¹¹You will be enriched in every way for your great generosity, which will produce thanksgiving to God through us; ¹²for the rendering of this ministry not only

supplies the needs of the saints but also overflows with many thanksgivings to God. [13]Through the testing of this ministry you glorify God by your obedience to the confession of the gospel of Christ and by the generosity of your sharing with them and with all others, [14]while they long for you and pray for you because of the surpassing grace of God that he has given you. [15]Thanks be to God for his indescribable gift! *(2 Corinthians 9:6–15)*

REFLECT

What word or phrase "speaks" to you in this passage? Record here:

Draw a picture or symbol of what you have discovered this time. If you prefer, act out some motion that expresses it.

What don't you feel you have enough of? Ask God about this and listen to God's response.

PRAY

Write or draw a prayer if you like.

RESPOND

To what response is God calling you?

Day Three

Rest*

Lord, open unto me
    Open unto me—light for my darkness.
    Open unto me—courage for my fear.
    Open unto me—hope for my despair.
    Open unto me—peace for my turmoil.
    Open unto me—joy for my sorrow.
    Open unto me—strength for my weakness.
    Open unto me—wisdom for my confusion.
    Open unto me—forgiveness for my sin.
    Open unto me—love for my hates.
    Open unto me—thy Self for my self.
Lord, Lord, open unto me!

Howard Thurman

*Option: Use favorite art or Taize music for resting.

Read and Reflect

⁶The point is this: the one who sows sparingly will also reap sparingly, and the one who sows bountifully will also reap bountifully. ⁷Each of you must give as you have made up your mind, not reluctantly or under compulsion, for God loves a cheerful giver. ⁸And God is able to provide you with every blessing in abundance, so that by always having enough of everything, you may share abundantly in every good work. ⁹As it is written, "He scatters abroad, he gives to the poor; his righteousness endures forever." ¹⁰He who supplies seed to the sower and bread for food will supply and multiply your seed for sowing and increase the harvest of your righteousness. ¹¹You will be enriched in every way for your great generosity, which will produce thanksgiving to God through us; ¹²for the rendering of this ministry not

only supplies the needs of the saints but also overflows with many thanksgivings to God. [13]Through the testing of this ministry you glorify God by your obedience to the confession of the gospel of Christ and by the generosity of your sharing with them and with all others, [14]while they long for you and pray for you because of the surpassing grace of God that he has given you. [15]Thanks be to God for his indescribable gift! *(2 Corinthians 9:6–15)*

REFLECT

What word or phrase "speaks" to you in this passage? Record here:

Imagine the word or phrase as a seed planted in you from the scripture you just read. Draw or act out how this seed is growing in you. What is God asking you to grow and harvest?

PRAY

Write or draw a prayer if you like.

RESPOND

To what response is God calling you?

Day Four

REST

Lord, open unto me
    Open unto me—light for my darkness.
    Open unto me—courage for my fear.
    Open unto me—hope for my despair.
    Open unto me—peace for my turmoil.
    Open unto me—joy for my sorrow.
    Open unto me—strength for my weakness.
    Open unto me—wisdom for my confusion.
    Open unto me—forgiveness for my sin.
    Open unto me—love for my hates.
    Open unto me—thy Self for my self.
Lord, Lord, open unto me!

Howard Thurman

READ AND REFLECT

[6]The point is this: the one who sows sparingly will also reap sparingly, and the one who sows bountifully will also reap bountifully. [7]Each of you must give as you have made up your mind, not reluctantly or under compulsion, for God loves a cheerful giver. [8]And God is able to provide you with every blessing in abundance, so that by always having enough of everything, you may share abundantly in every good work. [9]As it is written, "He scatters abroad, he gives to the poor; his righteousness endures forever." [10]He who supplies seed to the sower and bread for food will supply and multiply your seed for sowing and increase the harvest of your righteousness. [11]You will be enriched in every way for your great generosity, which will produce thanksgiving to God through us; [12]for the rendering of this ministry not only supplies the needs of the saints but also overflows

with many thanksgivings to God. [13]Through the testing of
this ministry you glorify God by your obedience to the
confession of the gospel of Christ and by the generosity of
your sharing with them and with all others, [14]while they
long for you and pray for you because of the surpassing
grace of God that he has given you. [15]Thanks be to God for
his indescribable gift! *(2 Corinthians 9:6–15)*

REFLECT

What word or phrase "speaks" to you in this passage? Record here:

Take the word or phrase that seems to "jump" at you today and
draw it with your hands in the air. You may also want to put this word
or phrase on this page in a color that seems appropriate.

What is your ministry? Is there a "test" in your ministry now?

PRAY

Write or draw a prayer if you like.

RESPOND

To what response is God calling you?

Day Five

REST

Lord, open unto me
>   Open unto me—light for my darkness.
>   Open unto me—courage for my fear.
>   Open unto me—hope for my despair.
>   Open unto me—peace for my turmoil.
>   Open unto me—joy for my sorrow.
>   Open unto me—strength for my weakness.
>   Open unto me—wisdom for my confusion.
>   Open unto me—forgiveness for my sin.
>   Open unto me—love for my hates.
>   Open unto me—thy Self for my self.
> Lord, Lord, open unto me!

Howard Thurman

READ AND REFLECT

⁶The point is this: the one who sows sparingly will also reap sparingly, and the one who sows bountifully will also reap bountifully. ⁷Each of you must give as you have made up your mind, not reluctantly or under compulsion, for God loves a cheerful giver. ⁸And God is able to provide you with every blessing in abundance, so that by always having enough of everything, you may share abundantly in every good work. ⁹As it is written, "He scatters abroad, he gives to the poor; his righteousness endures forever." ¹⁰He who supplies seed to the sower and bread for food will supply and multiply your seed for sowing and increase the harvest of your righteousness. ¹¹You will be enriched in every way for your great generosity, which will produce thanksgiving to God through us; ¹²for the rendering of this ministry not only supplies the needs of the saints but also overflows

with many thanksgivings to God. [13]Through the testing of this ministry you glorify God by your obedience to the confession of the gospel of Christ and by the generosity of your sharing with them and with all others, [14]while they long for you and pray for you because of the surpassing grace of God that he has given you. [15]Thanks be to God for his indescribable gift! *(2 Corinthians 9:6–15)*

REFLECT

What word or phrase "speaks" to you in this passage? Record here:

Imagine yourself taking the word or phrase that seems to "jump" at you today and embracing it as you would a child. What can this word or phrase teach you about yourself? About God's love for you?

How hard is it for you to hold onto that word or phrase for your life? Today, repeat it three or more times during the day as a reminder that God wants to equip you for this day with some blessing from that word or phrase.

PRAY

Write or draw a prayer if you like.

RESPOND

To what response is God calling you?

Day Six

Rest

Lord, open unto me
    Open unto me—light for my darkness.
    Open unto me—courage for my fear.
    Open unto me—hope for my despair.
    Open unto me—peace for my turmoil.
    Open unto me—joy for my sorrow.
    Open unto me—strength for my weakness.
    Open unto me—wisdom for my confusion.
    Open unto me—forgiveness for my sin.
    Open unto me—love for my hates.
    Open unto me—thy Self for my self.
Lord, Lord, open unto me!

Howard Thurman

Read and Reflect

[6]The point is this: the one who sows sparingly will also reap sparingly, and the one who sows bountifully will also reap bountifully. [7]Each of you must give as you have made up your mind, not reluctantly or under compulsion, for God loves a cheerful giver. [8]And God is able to provide you with every blessing in abundance, so that by always having enough of everything, you may share abundantly in every good work. [9]As it is written, "He scatters abroad, he gives to the poor; his righteousness endures forever." [10]He who supplies seed to the sower and bread for food will supply and multiply your seed for sowing and increase the harvest of your righteousness. [11]You will be enriched in every way for your great generosity, which will produce thanksgiving to God through us; [12]for the rendering of this ministry not only supplies the needs of the saints but also overflows

with many thanksgivings to God. [13]Through the testing of this ministry you glorify God by your obedience to the confession of the gospel of Christ and by the generosity of your sharing with them and with all others, [14]while they long for you and pray for you because of the surpassing grace of God that he has given you. [15]Thanks be to God for his indescribable gift! *(2 Corinthians 9:6–15)*

REFLECT

What word or phrase "speaks" to you in this passage? Record here:

Make a symbol for the word or phrase and either act out this symbol or record it on this page.

Thanksgiving is a way we show God our gratitude for God's work in and through us. List six things in life you are most thankful for. Praise God for them in song, dance, or poetry. Risk trying something new.

PRAY

Write or draw a prayer if you like.

RESPOND

To what response is God calling you?

Group Meeting Day

REST

The leader reads the following prayer and leaves time for silence.

Lord, open unto me
    Open unto me—light for my darkness.
    Open unto me—courage for my fear.
    Open unto me—hope for my despair.
    Open unto me—peace for my turmoil.
    Open unto me—joy for my sorrow.
    Open unto me—strength for my weakness.
    Open unto me—wisdom for my confusion.
    Open unto me—forgiveness for my sin.
    Open unto me—love for my hates.
    Open unto me—thy Self for my self.
Lord, Lord, open unto me!

Howard Thurman

READ AND REFLECT

The leader reads the passage aloud, followed by silence as group members listen for the word or phrase that resonates with them.

⁶The point is this: the one who sows sparingly will also reap sparingly, and the one who sows bountifully will also reap bountifully. ⁷Each of you must give as you have made up your mind, not reluctantly or under compulsion, for God loves a cheerful giver. ⁸And God is able to provide you with every blessing in abundance, so that by always having enough of everything, you may share abundantly in every good work. ⁹As it is written, "He scatters abroad, he gives

to the poor; his righteousness endures forever." [10]He who supplies seed to the sower and bread for food will supply and multiply your seed for sowing and increase the harvest of your righteousness. [11]You will be enriched in every way for your great generosity, which will produce thanksgiving to God through us; [12]for the rendering of this ministry not only supplies the needs of the saints but also overflows with many thanksgivings to God. [13]Through the testing of this ministry you glorify God by your obedience to the confession of the gospel of Christ and by the generosity of your sharing with them and with all others, [14]while they long for you and pray for you because of the surpassing grace of God that he has given you. [15]Thanks be to God for his indescribable gift! *(2 Corinthians 9:6–15)*

REFLECT

What word or phrase "speaks" to you in this passage? Record here:

Each person shares a day this week that was helpful, challenging, or puzzling, in the devotional reading. All are encouraged to share creative pieces if they like.

PRAY

Have each member of the group thank God for an indescribable gift he or she has received from God.

RESPOND

To what response is God calling you? Close the meeting by singing "Harvest of Righteousness" on page vii.

Additional Reflection Selections

Bread of Heaven, On Thee We Feed

Bread of heaven, on Thee we feed, for Thou art our food
  indeed,
Ever may our souls be fed with this true and living bread,
Day by day with strength supplied, through the life of Christ
  who died.

Vine of heaven, thy love supplies, this blest cup of sacrifice,
'Tis Thy wounds our healing give, to Thy cross we look and
  live:
Thou our life! O let us be rooted, grafted, built on Thee.

Josiah Conder, 1824

From Hildegard of Bingen:

For the soul passes through the body just as sap passes
through a tree. What does it mean? It is through the sap
that the tree is green, produces flowers, and then fruit.
And how does the fruit come to maturity? The sun warms
it, the rain waters it, and it is perfected by the mildness of
the air. The mercy of the grace of God will make a person
bright as the sun, the breadth of the Holy Spirit will lead
the person to the perfection of good fruits just like the
mildness of the air does for the tree (Uhlein 55).

The Shorter Catechism

What is the chief end of humankind?
  The chief end of humankind is to glorify God and enjoy
  God forever.

For through the spirit, by faith, we eagerly wait for the
hope of righteousness. *(Galatians 5:5)*

The best prayers are often more groans than words.

John Bunyan

It may be our imaginative creativity, which is always char-
acterized by a sense of play, that really makes us human.

Morton Kelsey

If the only prayer in your whole life is "thank you," that
would suffice. Meister Eckhart

When you pray, you open yourself to the influence of the
power which has revealed itself as love. That power gives
you freedom and independence. Once touched by this
Power you are no longer swayed back and forth by the
countless opinions, ideas and feelings which flow through
you. You have found a CENTER for your life, a center that
gives you the creative distance so that everything you see,
hear and feel can be tested against the source. (Nouwen
1972, 120)

On using scripture for devotional reading:

Here take such instructions as readily present themselves to your thoughts, repeat them over to your own con-
science, and charge your heart religiously to observe them,
and act upon them under the sense of the divine authority
which attends them. And if you pray over the substance of
this scripture, with your Bible open before you, it may
impress your memory and your heart yet more deeply, and
may form you to a copiousness and variety both of
thoughts and expression in prayer. (Doddridge n.d., 189)

We Plow the Fields and Scatter

We plow the fields and scatter The good seed on the land,
But it is fed and watered By God's almighty hand;
God sends the snow in winter, The warmth to swell the
    grain,
The breezes and the sunshine, And soft refreshing rain.

We thank You then, Creator, For all things bright and good,
The seedtime and the harvest, Our life, our health, our food;
Accept the gifts we offer, For all Your love imparts,
And what You most would welcome, Our humble, thankful
    hearts.   (*Presbyterian Hymnal*, no. 560)

From Some Thoughts Concerning the Revival:
True virtue or holiness has its seat chiefly in the heart
rather than the head.

                                Jonathan Edwards

On the necessity of prayer:
Words fail to explain how necessary prayer is, and in how
many ways the exercise of prayer is profitable.

                                (Baxter 1847)

RECORD YOUR OWN THOUGHTS AND REFLECTIONS HERE:

SPACE FOR RECORDING

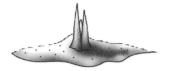

Week Two

Day One

Rest*

> O Lord, my heart is not lifted up,
>   my eyes are not raised too high;
> I do not occupy myself with things
>   too great and too marvelous for me.
> But I have calmed and quieted my soul,
>   like a weaned child with its mother;
>   my soul is like the weaned child that is with me.
> O Israel, hope in the Lord
>   from this time on and forevermore. *(Psalm 131)*

*Option: Use selected art or Taize music for resting.

Read and Reflect

Parable of the Mustard Seed

³⁰He also said, "With what can we compare the kingdom of God, or what parable will we use for it? ³¹It is like a mustard seed, which, when sown upon the ground, is the smallest of all the seeds on earth; ³²yet when it is sown it grows up and becomes the greatest of all shrubs, and puts forth large branches, so that the birds of the air can make nests in its shade." *(Mark 4:30–32)*

Sow for yourselves righteousness; reap steadfast love; break up your fallow ground; for it is a time to seek the Lord that [God] may come and rain righteousness upon you. *(Hosea 10:12)*

REFLECT

What word or phrase "speaks" to you in these passages? Record here:

What is the fallow ground in your life that God is calling you to plant with righteousness and love?

Sometime today take one small step to stir your fallow ground. Make a sketch of how the ground is now and what you imagine it might look like as time goes on.

What is your place in the kingdom of God? What small seed are you to plant in this world today?

PRAY

Write or draw a prayer if you like.

RESPOND

To what response is God calling you?

Day Two

REST

> O Lord, my heart is not lifted up,
>> my eyes are not raised too high;
> I do not occupy myself with things
>> too great and too marvelous for me.
> But I have calmed and quieted my soul,
>> like a weaned child with its mother;
>>> my soul is like the weaned child that is with me.
> O Israel, hope in the LORD
>> from this time on and forevermore. *(Psalm 131)*

READ AND REFLECT

Parable of the Mustard Seed

³⁰He also said, "With what can we compare the kingdom of God, or what parable will we use for it? ³¹It is like a mustard seed, which, when sown upon the ground, is the smallest of all the seeds on earth; ³²yet when it is sown it grows up and becomes the greatest of all shrubs, and puts forth large branches, so that the birds of the air can make nests in its shade." *(Mark 4:30–32)*

Sow for yourselves righteousness; reap steadfast love; break up your fallow ground; for it is a time to seek the LORD that [God] may come and rain righteousness upon you. *(Hosea 10:12)*

REFLECT

What word or phrase "speaks" to you in these passages? Record here:

Participating in the use of this workbook means you are "seeking the Lord" in your life. Name the one thing you are seeking today. Take this word or phrase, and write the letters of the word vertically down the side of a piece of paper. Make this into a prayer and stop at lunch and before dinner or at bedtime to remind yourself what it is that you are seeking of the Lord today. For example, if you are seeking love, you might write

L onging to be held by God

O pen to the seed of love to grow in me

V ery afraid of not growing—and not growing

E ver ready to let God love

PRAY

RESPOND

To what response is God calling you?

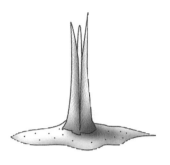

Day Three

REST

> O Lord, my heart is not lifted up,
>   my eyes are not raised too high;
> I do not occupy myself with things
>   too great and too marvelous for me.
> But I have calmed and quieted my soul,
>   like a weaned child with its mother;
>   my soul is like the weaned child that is with me.
> O Israel, hope in the LORD
>   from this time on and forevermore. *(Psalm 131)*

READ AND REFLECT

Parable of the Mustard Seed

³⁰He also said, "With what can we compare the kingdom of God, or what parable will we use for it? ³¹It is like a mustard seed, which, when sown upon the ground, is the smallest of all the seeds on earth; ³²yet when it is sown it grows up and becomes the greatest of all shrubs, and puts forth large branches, so that the birds of the air can make nests in its shade." *(Mark 4:30–32)*

Sow for yourselves righteousness; reap steadfast love; break up your fallow ground; for it is a time to seek the LORD that [God] may come and rain righteousness upon you. *(Hosea 10:12)*

REFLECT

What word or phrase "speaks" to you in these passages? Record here:

If the kingdom of God is where God rules, what place in your life are you seeking to let the seed of God's love grow for you? God desires the kingdom in your life. Make a four-part sketch showing how the stages of growth might be: from the seed you choose with God's help to grow to the sprouting, the development, and the fruit of the seed.

PRAY

RESPOND

To what response is God calling you?

Day Four

REST

> O Lord, my heart is not lifted up,
>   my eyes are not raised too high;
> I do not occupy myself with things
>   too great and too marvelous for me.
> But I have calmed and quieted my soul,
>   like a weaned child with its mother;
>   my soul is like the weaned child that is with me.
> O Israel, hope in the LORD
>   from this time on and forevermore. *(Psalm 131)*

READ AND REFLECT

Parable of the Mustard Seed

³⁰He also said, "With what can we compare the kingdom of God, or what parable will we use for it? ³¹It is like a mustard seed, which, when sown upon the ground, is the smallest of all the seeds on earth; ³²yet when it is sown it grows up and becomes the greatest of all shrubs, and puts forth large branches, so that the birds of the air can make their nest in its shade." *(Mark 4:30–32)*

Sow for yourselves righteousness; reap steadfast love; break up your fallow ground; for it is a time to seek the LORD that [God] may come and rain righteousness upon you. *(Hosea 10:12)*

REFLECT

What word or phrase "speaks" to you in these passages? Record here:

Today, sit quietly with the word or phrase that seemed to reach out to you in scripture. Imagine holding that word in the palm of your hand. Observe what happens, and record it in music, poetry, or drawing—or whatever way seems fitting to you.

PRAY

RESPOND

To what response is God calling you?

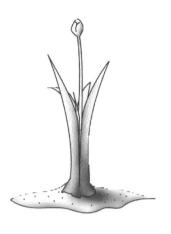

Day Five

Rest

O Lord, my heart is not lifted up,
    my eyes are not raised too high;
I do not occupy myself with things
    too great and too marvelous for me.
But I have calmed and quieted my soul,
    like a weaned child with its mother;
    my soul is like the weaned child that is with me.
O Israel, hope in the Lord
    from this time on and forevermore. *(Psalm 131)*

Read and Reflect

Parable of the Mustard Seed

[30]He also said, "With what can we compare the kingdom of God, or what parable will we use for it? [31]It is like a mustard seed, which, when sown upon the ground, is the smallest of all the seeds on earth; [32]yet when it is sown it grows up and becomes the greatest of all shrubs, and puts forth large branches, so that the birds of the air can make nests in its shade." *(Mark 4:30–32)*

Sow for yourselves righteousness; reap steadfast love; break up your fallow ground; for it is a time to seek the Lord that [God] may come and rain righteousness upon you. *(Hosea 10:12)*

REFLECT

What word or phrase "speaks" to you in these passages? Record here:

Growth is a slow process. Is there a place in your mustard seed faith where you need patience? God promises to rain righteousness upon you, and part of that righteousness is patience for God's activity in your life. Sit quietly and imagine letting the gentle rain of God fall on you. What color is it? Does it have a special texture? How does it make you feel? If you like, name the feeling and put it on a piece of paper or a 3- x 5-inch card and carry it with you today as a reminder that you are God's seed in the making.

PRAY

RESPOND

To what response is God calling you?

Day Six

REST

> O Lord, my heart is not lifted up,
>   my eyes are not raised too high;
> I do not occupy myself with things
>   too great and too marvelous for me.
> But I have calmed and quieted my soul,
>   like a weaned child with its mother;
>   my soul is like the weaned child that is with me.
> O Israel, hope in the LORD
>   from this time on and forevermore. *(Psalm 131)*

READ AND REFLECT

Parable of the Mustard Seed

³⁰He also said, "With what can we compare the kingdom of God, or what parable will we use for it? ³¹It is like a mustard seed, which, when sown upon the ground, is the smallest of all the seeds on earth; ³²yet when it is sown it grows up and becomes the greatest of all shrubs, and puts forth large branches, so that the birds of the air can make nests in its shade." *(Mark 4:30–32)*

Sow for yourselves righteousness; reap steadfast love; break up your fallow ground; for it is a time to seek the LORD that [God] may come and rain righteousness upon you. *(Hosea 10:12)*

REFLECT

What word or phrase "speaks" to you in these passages? Record here:

For reflection, use one of the additional readings for Week Two or the word or phrase that was significant for you today. What is the invitation here to encourage God's growth in you? Are you reminded of a Bible story that you want to explore? Find that story and read it.

PRAY

RESPOND

To what response is God calling you?

Group Meeting Day

REST

Begin by resting in Psalm 131, reading it in unison, followed by silence. The leader asks the people to put their names in the blank.

> O Lord, my heart is not lifted up,
> my eyes are not raised too high;
> I do not occupy myself with things
>   too great and too marvelous for me.
> But I have calmed and quieted my soul,
>   like a weaned child with its mother;
>   my soul is like the weaned child that is with me.
> O _____, hope in the LORD
>   from this time on and forevermore.

READ AND REFLECT

The leader reads the passages aloud, followed by silence as group members listen for the word or phrase that resonates with them.

Parable of the Mustard Seed

[30]He also said, "With what can we compare the kingdom of God, or what parable will we use for it? [31]It is like a mustard seed, which, when sown upon the ground, is the smallest of all the seeds on earth; [32]yet when it is sown it grows up and becomes the greatest of all shrubs, and puts forth large branches, so that the birds of the air can make nests in its shade." *(Mark 4:30–32)*

Sow for yourselves righteousness; reap steadfast love; break up your fallow ground; for it is a time to seek the LORD that [God] may come and rain righteousness upon you.

(Hosea 10:12)

REFLECT

What word or phrase "speaks" to you in these passages? Record here:

Have group members share today's word or phrase or a day that was meaningful to them.

PRAY

After each person shares, the person to the right prays for that individual, remembering in prayer what has been shared.

RESPOND

To what response is God calling you as you reflect on the last week? Share this with the group. This week's group meeting closes by singing "Water Our Lives" from page 48.

Additional Reflection Selections

When the Lord restored the fortunes of Zion,
   we were like those who dream.
Then our mouth was filled with laughter,
   and our tongue with shouts of joy;
then it was said among the nations,
   "The LORD has done great things for them."
The Lord has done great things for us,
   and we rejoiced.
Restore our fortunes, O LORD,
   like the watercourses in the Negeb.
May those who sow in tears
   reap with shouts of joy.
Those who go out weeping,
   bearing the seed for sowing,
shall come home with shouts of joy,
   carrying their sheaves.

(Psalm 126)

Most Christians are convinced that prayer is more than the outward performance of an obligation, in which we tell God things he already knows. It is more than a kind of daily waiting in attendance on the exalted Sovereign who receives his subjects' homage morning and evening. And although many Christians experience in pain and regret that their prayer gets no further than this lowly stage, they are sure, nonetheless, that there should be more to it. In this field there lies a hidden treasure, if only I could find it and dig it up. This seed has the power to become a mighty tree bearing blossoms and fruit, if only I would plant and tend it. This hard and distasteful duty would yield the freest and most blessed kind of life, if only I could open and surrender myself to it. Christians know this, or at least they have an obscure intimation of it on the basis of prior experiences of one kind or another, but they have never dared to follow these beckoning paths and enter the land

of promise. The birds of the air have eaten up the sown word, the thorns of everyday life have choked it; all that remains of it is a vague regret in the soul. And if, at particular times throughout life, they feel an urgent need for a relationship with God which is different from the incessant repetition of set prayers, they feel clumsy and lacking in ability, as if they had to speak in a language without having mastered its grammar. Instead of fluent conversation they can only manage a few, halting scraps of the heavenly idiom. Like a stranger in a foreign land, unacquainted with the language, they are almost inarticulate children once again, wanting to say something but unable to do so.
(von Balthasar 1986, 13)

Blessed are those who hunger and thirst for righteousness,
for they will be filled.
Blessed are those who are persecuted for righteousness' sake,
for theirs is the kingdom of heaven. *(Matthew 5:6, 10)*

Walking can be a wonderful contemplative exercise.
William Johnson

    The spirit of the Lord GOD is upon me,
because the LORD has anointed me;
he has sent me to bring good news to the oppressed,
   to bind up the brokenhearted,
to proclaim liberty to the captives,
   and release to the prisoners;
to proclaim the year of the LORD's favor,
   and the day of vengeance of our God;
   to comfort all who mourn,
to provide for those who mourn in Zion—
   to give them a garland instead of ashes,
the oil of gladness instead of mourning,
   the mantle of praise instead of a faint spirit.
They will be called oaks of righteousness,
   the planting of the LORD, to display his glory.
(Isaiah 61:1–3)

From Hildegard of Bingen:

> Under your protection, I rejoice, O God!
> In Your shadow, I exult, O God!
> You rescue me from the heaviness of sin.
> My soul anticipates drawing ever closer to you
> in the doing of good works.
> This supreme longing pulls me to you,
> beckons me come under your protection,
> into the shadow of your power.
> I am secure from all enemies there!
>
> The first seed of the longing for Justice
> blows through the soul like the wind.
> The taste for good will play in it like a breeze.
>
> The consummation of this seed is a greening of the soul
> that is like that of the ripening world.
> Now the soul honors God by the doing of just deeds.
> The soul is only as strong as its work. (Uhlein 1982, 123)

Symbols of our inner truth may be images, happenings, objects or sound; they may be noticed in dreams, in art forms or in the most ordinary experiences. Whatever their form, they express a profound meaning that is beyond the grasp of words.

Carol Marie Kelly

From *Meditations with Julian of Norwich* by Brendan Doyle, 1983:

"That which is impossible for you is not impossible to me: I will preserve my word in all things and I will make all things well." The fullness of joy is to behold God in everything. God is the ground, the substance, the teaching, the teacher, the purpose, and the reward for which every soul labors. True thanking is to enjoy God. Thanking is a true understanding of who we really are. With reverence and awe we turn ourselves around towards the working that our good God incites in us to do, enjoying and thanking with our real selves.

The Harvest of the Heart

This is the season of gathering in, the season of the harvest in nature. Many things that are started in spring and early summer have grown to fruition and are now ready for reaping. Great and significant as is the harvest in nature, the most pertinent kind of ingathering for the human spirit is what I call "the harvest of the heart." Long ago, Jesus said that men should not lay up for themselves treasures on earth where moths corrupt and thieves break in and steal, but that men should lay up for themselves treasures in heaven. This insight suggests that life consists of planting and harvesting, of sowing and reaping. We are always in the midst of the harvest and always in the midst of planting. The words that we use in communication, the profound stirrings of the mind out of which thoughts and ideas arise, the ebb and flow of desires out of which the simple or complex deeds develops, are all caught in the process of reaping and sowing, of planting and harvesting. There are no anonymous deeds, no casual processes. Living is a shared process. Even as I am conscious of things growing in me planted by others, which things are always ripening, so others are conscious of things growing in them planted by me, which are always ripening. Inasmuch as I do not live or die unto myself, it is of the essence of wisdom for me conscientiously to live and die in the profound awareness of other people. The statement, "Know thyself," has been taken mystically from the statement, "Thou hast seen thy brother, thou has seen thy God."

Howard Thurman

WATER OUR LIVES

Andy Dreitcer

Joy Luscombe

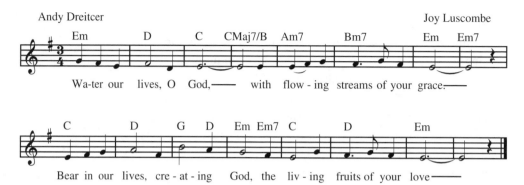

Wa-ter our lives, O God,—— with flow-ing streams of your grace.——

Bear in our lives, cre-at-ing God, the liv-ing fruits of your love———

RECORD YOUR OWN THOUGHTS AND REFLECTIONS HERE:

Space for Recording

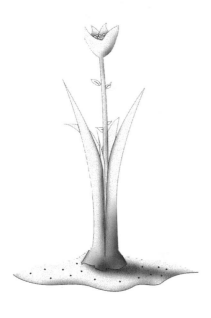

Week Three

Day One

REST

O God, full of compassion,
I commit and commend myself to you,
in whom I am, and live, and know.
Be the goal of my pilgrimage, and the rest by the way.
Let my soul take refuge from the crowding turmoil
    of worldly thought
beneath the shadow of your wings.
Let my heart, this sea of restless waves,
find peace in you, O God.

Augustine of Hippo (354–430)

READ AND REFLECT

[10]For as the rain and the snow come down from heaven,
    and do not return there until they have watered the earth,
making it bring forth and sprout,
    giving seed to the sower and bread to the eater,
[11]so shall my word be that goes out from my mouth;
    it shall not return to me empty,
but it shall accomplish that which I purpose,
    and succeed in the thing for which I sent it.
[12]For you shall go out in joy, and be led back in peace;

(Isaiah 55:10–12a)

[18]"Hear then the parable of the sower. [19]When anyone hears the word of the kingdom and does not understand it, the evil one comes and snatches away what is sown in the heart; this is what was sown on the path. [20]As for what was sown on rocky ground, this is the one who hears the word

and immediately receives it with joy; [21]yet such a person has no root, but endures only for a while, and when trouble or persecution arises on account of the word, that person immediately falls away. [22]As for what was sown among thorns, this is the one who hears the word but the cares of the world and the lure of wealth choke the word, and it yields nothing. [23]But as for what was sown on good soil, this is the one who hears the word and understands it, who indeed bears fruit and yields, in one case a hundredfold, in another sixty, and in another thirty." *(Matthew 13:18-23)*

REFLECT

What word or phrase "speaks" to you in these passages? Record here:

The Word of God is like a seed. What seed is God giving you? Imagine what the seed looks like—its color—its case. What will it take for it to break open and grow? Use your whole body to express this slow sprouting of this seed in you.

Read more of Matthew 13—noting Matthew 13:43 in particular.

PRAY

RESPOND

To what response is God calling you?

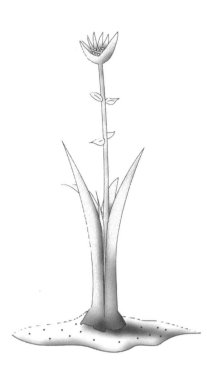

Day Two

REST

O God, full of compassion,
I commit and commend myself to you,
in whom I am, and live, and know.
Be the goal of my pilgrimage, and the rest by the way.
Let my soul take refuge from the crowding turmoil
   of worldly thought
beneath the shadow of your wings.
Let my heart, this sea of restless waves,
find peace in you, O God.

                      Augustine of Hippo (354–430)

READ AND REFLECT

[10]For as the rain and the snow come down from heaven,
   and do not return there until they have watered the earth,
making it bring forth and sprout,
   giving seed to the sower and bread to the eater,
[11]so shall my word be that goes out from my mouth;
   it shall not return to me empty,
but it shall accomplish that which I purpose,
   and succeed in the thing for which I sent it.
[12]For you shall go out in joy, and be led back in peace;

                      (Isaiah 55:10–12a)

[18]"Hear then the parable of the sower. [19]When anyone hears the word of the kingdom and does not understand it, the evil one comes and snatches away what is sown in the heart; this is what was sown on the path. [20]As for what was sown on rocky ground, this is the one who hears the word and immediately receives it with joy; [21]yet such a person has no root, but endures only for a while, and when trouble or persecution arises on account of the word, that person

immediately falls away. 22As for what was sown among thorns, this is the one who hears the word but the cares of the world and the lure of wealth choke the word, and it yields nothing. 23But as for what was sown on good soil, this is the one who hears the word and understands it, who indeed bears fruit and yields, in one case a hundredfold, in another sixty, and in another thirty." *(Matthew 13:18–23)*

REFLECT

What word or phrase "speaks" to you in these passages? Record here:

Nourishment of the seed is important. What do you need to nourish the seed of God's word in you? Ask God for that in prayer. Imagine this seed as it produces some kind of fruit that will be yielded in God's time. Write the word or phrase or draw a picture to signify this fruit. How are you called to share this fruit with others?

PRAY

RESPOND

To what response is God calling you?

Day Three

REST

O God, full of compassion,
I commit and commend myself to you,
in whom I am, and live, and know.
Be the goal of my pilgrimage, and the rest by the way.
Let my soul take refuge from the crowding turmoil
    of worldly thought
beneath the shadow of your wings.
Let my heart, this sea of restless waves,
find peace in you, O God.

Augustine of Hippo (354–430)

READ AND REFLECT

[10]For as the rain and the snow come down from heaven,
    and do not return there until they have watered the earth,
making it bring forth and sprout,
    giving seed to the sower and bread to the eater,
[11]so shall my word be that goes out from my mouth;
    it shall not return to me empty,
but it shall accomplish that which I purpose,
    and succeed in the thing for which I sent it.
[12]For you shall go out in joy, and be led back in peace;

(Isaiah 55:10–12a)

[18]"Hear then the parable of the sower. [19]When anyone hears the word of the kingdom and does not understand it, the evil one comes and snatches away what is sown in the heart; this is what was sown on the path. [20]As for what was sown on rocky ground, this is the one who hears the word and immediately receives it with joy; [21]yet such a person has no root, but endures only for a while, and when trouble or persecution arises on account of the word, that person

immediately falls away. ²²As for what was sown among thorns, this is the one who hears the word but the cares of the world and the lure of wealth choke the word, and it yields nothing. ²³But as for what was sown on good soil, this is the one who hears the word and understands it, who indeed bears fruit and yields, in one case a hundredfold, in another sixty, and in another thirty." *(Matthew 13:18–23)*

REFLECT

What word or phrase "speaks" to you in these passages? Record here:

How does this word or phrase (or another one drawn from Week Three's "Additional Reflection Selections") bring you joy and peace from God? As you go about your day, think back to this time, and let that same peace and joy be part of your living out this day. You might want to make a symbol of this joy and peace and place the symbol where you will see it.

PRAY

RESPOND

To what response is God calling you?

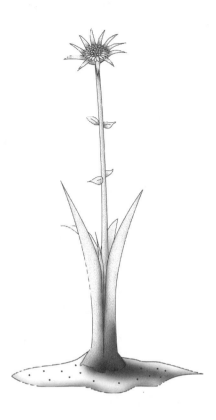

Day Four

Rest

O God, full of compassion,
I commit and commend myself to you,
in whom I am, and live, and know.
Be the goal of my pilgrimage, and the rest by the way.
Let my soul take refuge from the crowding turmoil
    of worldly thought
beneath the shadow of your wings.
Let my heart, this sea of restless waves,
find peace in you, O God.

Augustine of Hippo (354–430)

Read and Reflect

[10]For as the rain and the snow come down from heaven,
    and do not return there until they have watered the earth,
making it bring forth and sprout,
    giving seed to the sower and bread to the eater,
[11]so shall my word be that goes out from my mouth;
    it shall not return to me empty,
but it shall accomplish that which I purpose,
    and succeed in the thing for which I sent it.
[12]For you shall go out in joy, and be led back in peace;

(Isaiah 55:10–12a)

[18]"Hear then the parable of the sower. [19]When anyone hears the word of the kingdom and does not understand it, the evil one comes and snatches away what is sown in the heart; this is what was sown on the path. [20]As for what was sown on rocky ground, this is the one who hears the word and immediately receives it with joy; [21]yet such a person has no root, but endures only for a while, and when trouble or persecution arises on account of the word, that person

immediately falls away. ²²As for what was sown among thorns, this is the one who hears the word but the cares of the world and the lure of wealth choke the word, and it yields nothing. ²³But as for what was sown on good soil, this is the one who hears the word and understands it, who indeed bears fruit and yields, in one case a hundredfold, in another sixty, and in another thirty." *(Matthew 13:18–23)*

REFLECT

What word or phrase "speaks" to you in these passages? Record here:

Imagine this seed as it produces some kind of "bread" (some fruit that will be yielded in God's time). Write the word or phrase or draw a picture to signify the "bread." How are you called to share this "bread" with others?

PRAY

RESPOND

To what response is God calling you?

Day Five

REST

> O God, full of compassion,
> I commit and commend myself to you,
> in whom I am, and live, and know.
> Be the goal of my pilgrimage, and the rest by the way.
> Let my soul take refuge from the crowding turmoil
>   of worldly thought
> beneath the shadow of your wings.
> Let my heart, this sea of restless waves,
> find peace in you, O God.
>
> Augustine of Hippo (354–430)

READ AND REFLECT

> [10]For as the rain and the snow come down from heaven,
>   and do not return there until they have watered the earth,
> making it bring forth and sprout,
>   giving seed to the sower and bread to the eater,
> [11]so shall my word be that goes out from my mouth;
>   it shall not return to me empty,
> but it shall accomplish that which I purpose,
>   and succeed in the thing for which I sent it.
> [12]For you shall go out in joy, and be led back in peace;
>
> (Isaiah 55:10–12a)

[18]"Hear then the parable of the sower. [19]When anyone hears the word of the kingdom and does not understand it, the evil one comes and snatches away what is sown in the heart; this is what was sown on the path. [20]As for what was sown on rocky ground, this is the one who hears the word and immediately receives it with joy; [21]yet such a person has no root, but endures only for a while, and when trouble or persecution arises on account of the word, that person

immediately falls away. ²²As for what was sown among thorns, this is the one who hears the word but the cares of the world and the lure of wealth choke the word, and it yields nothing. ²³But as for what was sown on good soil, this is the one who hears the word and understands it, who indeed bears fruit and yields, in one case a hundredfold, in another sixty, and in another thirty." *(Matthew 13:18–23)*

REFLECT

What word or phrase "speaks" to you in these passages? Record here:

Of all the "seeds" that have stood out for you in the Word this week, which is most in danger because it has no root? Which is most at risk of being overcome by the cares and lures of the world? What do you need from God to support this fragile seed from the Word? Imagine yourself as you go about your day having all the support from God you need. How do you show God thankfulness for the rocky soil as well as the good soil?

PRAY

RESPOND

To what response is God calling you?

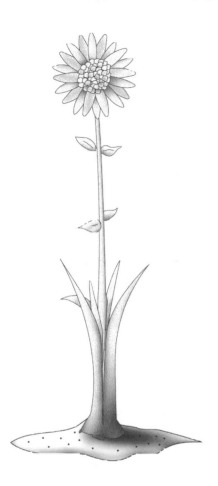

Day Six

Rest

O God, full of compassion,
I commit and commend myself to you,
in whom I am, and live, and know.
Be the goal of my pilgrimage, and the rest by the way.
Let my soul take refuge from the crowding turmoil
   of worldly thought
beneath the shadow of your wings.
Let my heart, this sea of restless waves,
find peace in you, O God.

Augustine of Hippo (354–430)

Read and Reflect

[10]For as the rain and the snow come down from heaven,
   and do not return there until they have watered the earth,
making it bring forth and sprout,
   giving seed to the sower and bread to the eater,
[11]so shall my word be that goes out from my mouth;
   it shall not return to me empty,
but it shall accomplish that which I purpose,
   and succeed in the thing for which I sent it.
[12]For you shall go out in joy, and be led back in peace;

(Isaiah 55:10–12a)

[18]"Hear then the parable of the sower. [19]When anyone hears the word of the kingdom and does not understand it, the evil one comes and snatches away what is sown in the heart; this is what was sown on the path. [20]As for what was sown on rocky ground, this is the one who hears the word and immediately receives it with joy; [21]yet such a person has no root, but endures only for a while, and when trouble or persecution arises on account of the word, that person

immediately falls away. [22]As for what was sown among thorns, this is the one who hears the word but the cares of the world and the lure of wealth choke the word, and it yields nothing. [23]But as for what was sown on good soil, this is the one who hears the word and understands it, who indeed bears fruit and yields, in one case a hundredfold, in another sixty, and in another thirty." *(Matthew 13:18–23)*

REFLECT

What word or phrase "speaks" to you in these passages? Record here:

Draw, write, or give body language to the word or phrase you believe God desires for you to bear fruit in abundance in your life.

PRAY

RESPOND

To what response is God calling you?

Group Meeting Day

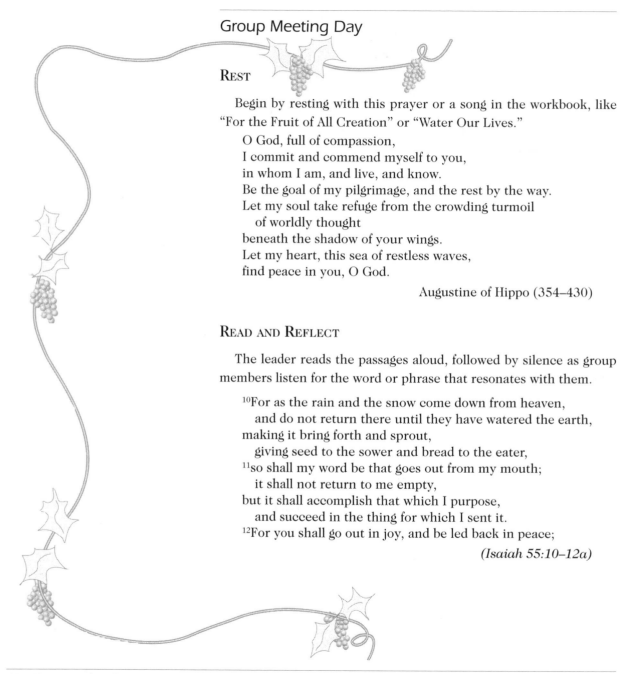

Rest

Begin by resting with this prayer or a song in the workbook, like "For the Fruit of All Creation" or "Water Our Lives."

O God, full of compassion,
I commit and commend myself to you,
in whom I am, and live, and know.
Be the goal of my pilgrimage, and the rest by the way.
Let my soul take refuge from the crowding turmoil
    of worldly thought
beneath the shadow of your wings.
Let my heart, this sea of restless waves,
find peace in you, O God.

Augustine of Hippo (354–430)

Read and Reflect

The leader reads the passages aloud, followed by silence as group members listen for the word or phrase that resonates with them.

[10]For as the rain and the snow come down from heaven,
    and do not return there until they have watered the earth,
making it bring forth and sprout,
    giving seed to the sower and bread to the eater,
[11]so shall my word be that goes out from my mouth;
    it shall not return to me empty,
but it shall accomplish that which I purpose,
    and succeed in the thing for which I sent it.
[12]For you shall go out in joy, and be led back in peace;

(Isaiah 55:10–12a)

¹⁸"Hear then the parable of the sower. ¹⁹When anyone hears the word of the kingdom and does not understand it, the evil one comes and snatches away what is sown in the heart; this is what was sown on the path. ²⁰As for what was sown on rocky ground, this is the one who hears the word and immediately receives it with joy; ²¹yet such a person has no root, but endures only for a while, and when trouble or persecution arises on account of the word, that person immediately falls away. ²²As for what was sown among thorns, this is the one who hears the word but the cares of the world and the lure of wealth choke the word, and it yields nothing. ²³But as for what was sown on good soil, this is the one who hears the word and understands it, who indeed bears fruit and yields, in one case a hundredfold, in another sixty, and in another thirty." *(Matthew 13:18–23)*

REFLECT

What word or phrase "speaks" to you in these passages? Record here:

Group members choose a day that they would like to share from the week and answer the question, What has your rootedness yielded for God? What has rootedness yielded for you?

PRAY

As a group, pray for ears to hear God's word and act on it. Have the prayer partner of each person name specific joys and concerns the partner desires as he or she grows as "a harvest of righteousness" for God.

RESPOND

To what response is God calling you?

Additional Reflection Selections

Commit your way to the LORD;
    trust in him, and he will act. *(Psalm 37:5)*

Steadfast love and faithfulness will meet;
    righteousness and peace will kiss each other.
Faithfulness will spring up from the ground,
    and righteousness will look down from the sky.
The LORD will give what is good,
    and our land will yield its increase.
Righteousness will go before him,
    and will make a path for his steps. *(Psalm 85:10–13)*

For the Fruit of All Creation

For the fruit of all creation, Thanks be to God.
For the gifts of every nation, Thanks be to God.
For the plowing, sowing, reaping, Silent growth while we are
    sleeping,
Future needs in earth's safekeeping, Thanks be to God.

In the just reward of labor, God's will be done.
In the help we give our neighbor, God's will be done.
In our worldwide task of caring For the hungry and despairing,
In the harvests we are sharing, God's will be done.

For the harvests of the Spirit, Thanks be to God.
For the good we all inherit, Thanks be to God.
For the wonders that astound us, For the truths that still
    confound us,
Most of all that love has found us, Thanks be to God.

       Fred Pratt Green, 1970 (*Presbyterian Hymnal*, no. 553)

Art enables us to find and lose ourselves at the same time. The mind that responds to the intellectual and spiritual values that lie hidden in a poem, a painting, or a piece of music, discovers a spiritual vitality that lifts it above itself, takes it out of itself, and makes it present to itself on a level of being that it did not know it could ever achieve.

Thomas Merton

15"Beware of false prophets, who come to you in sheep's clothing but inwardly are ravenous wolves. 16You will know them by their fruits. Are grapes gathered from thorns, or figs from thistles? 17In the same way, every good tree bears good fruit, but the bad tree bears bad fruit. 18A good tree cannot bear bad fruit, nor can a bad tree bear good fruit. 19Every tree that does not bear good fruit is cut down and thrown into the fire. 20Thus you will know them by their fruits." *(Matthew 7:15–20)*

Come, Sing a Song of Harvest

Come, sing a song of harvest, of thanks for daily food!
To offer God the firstfruits is old as gratitude.

Shall we, sometimes forgetful of where creations starts,
View science as our savior, lose wonder from our hearts?

May God, the great Creator, to whom all life belongs,
Accept these gifts we offer, our service and our songs.

And lest the world go hungry while we ourselves we fed,
Make each of us more ready to share our daily bread.

Fred Pratt Green, 1976 (*Presbyterian Hymnal*, no. 558)

Either make the tree good, and its fruit good; or make the tree bad, and its fruit bad; for the tree is known by its fruit. *(Matthew 12:33–34)*

From Hildegard of Bingen, pp. 49, 66, and 127:

Without the WORD of God
No creature has being,
God's WORD is in all creation, visible and invisible.
The WORD is living, being, spirit, all verdant greening, all
    creativity.
All creation is awakened, called, by the resounding melody,
God's invocation is the WORD.

The WORD is manifest in every creature.
Now this is how the spirit is in the flesh—
the WORD is indivisible from GOD.

The more one learns about that which one knows nothing of,
the more one gains in wisdom.
One has, therefore, through science,
eyes with which it behooves us to pay attention.

Who are the prophets?
They are a royal people, who penetrate mystery and
    see with the spirit's eyes.
In illuminating darkness they speak out.
They are living, penetrating clarity.
They are a blossom blooming only on the shoot that is
    rooted in the flood of light.

From Hildegard of Bingen, p. 31:

I am the One whose praise echoes on high.
I adorn all the earth.
I am the Breeze that nurtures all things green.
I encourage blossoms to flourish with ripening fruits.
I am led by the spirit to feed.
I am the rain coming from the dew that causes the grass to
    laugh with the joy of life.
I call forth tears, the aroma of holy work.
I am the yearning for good.

Darkness teaches us to listen.
> Rebecca Bradburn Langer

The seed of God is in us. Given an intelligent and hard-working farmer, it will thrive and grow up to God, whose seed it is; and accordingly its fruits will be God-nature. Pear seeds grow into pear seeds, nut seeds into nut seeds, and God seed into God.
> Meister Eckhart

Whatsoever a Man Soweth

I watched him for a long time. He was so busily engaged in his task that he did not notice my approach until he heard my voice. Then he raised himself erect with all the slow dignity of a man who had exhausted the cup of haste to the very dregs. He was an old man—as I discovered before our conversation was over, a full eighty-one years. Further talk between us revealed that he was planting a small grove of pecan trees. The little treelets were not more than two and a half or three feet in height. My curiosity was unbounded.

"Why did you not select larger trees so as to increase the possibility of your living to see them bear at least one cup of nuts?"

He fixed his eyes directly on my face, with no particular point of focus, but with a gaze that took in the totality of my features. Finally he said, "These small trees are cheaper and I have very little money."

"So you do not expect to live to see the trees reach sufficient maturity to bear fruit?"

"No, but is that important? All my life I have eaten fruit from trees that I did not plant, why should I not plant trees to bear fruit for those who may enjoy them long after I am gone? Besides, the man who plants because he will reap the harvest has no faith in life."

Howard Thurman

RECORD YOUR OWN THOUGHTS AND REFLECTIONS HERE:

Space for Recording

Week Four

Day One

REST*

God who plants the seed of love in our hearts,
I ask you to be with me in this time of rest.
Open my heart to receive all you want me to know.
May your Word burst to fulfillment
in the thoughts that I think, the words that I say,
    the deeds that I do.
May I be for you a harvest of righteousness yielding to your will
and empowered by your Word.
To God be all glory and praise, now and forever.

(Rebecca Bradburn Langer, 1995)

*Option: Use a favorite selection of art or Taize music for resting.

READ AND REFLECT

[3]I thank my God every time I remember you, [4]constantly praying with joy in every one of my prayers for all of you, [5]because of your sharing in the gospel from the first day until now. [6]I am confident of this, that the one who began a good work among you will bring it to completion by the day of Jesus Christ. [7]It is right for me to think this way about all of you, because you hold me in your heart, for all of you share in God's grace with me, both in my imprisonment and in the defense and confirmation of the gospel. [8]For God is my witness, how I long for all of you with the compassion of Christ Jesus. [9]And this is my prayer, that your love may overflow more and more with knowledge and full insight [10]to help you to determine what is best, so that in the day of

Christ you may be pure and blameless, [11]having produced
the harvest of righteousness that comes through Jesus
Christ for the glory and praise of God. *(Philippians 1:3–11)*

REFLECT

What word or phrase "speaks" to you in this passage? Record here:

Remember those people from childhood until now who helped
plant seeds of hope and faith in you. If possible write them a note of
thanks or write a prayer of thanksgiving in the workbook. Take a
walk. Every couple of steps name a person or occasion that deepened
the growth of your faith.

PRAY

RESPOND

To what response is God calling you?

Day Two

Rest

God who plants the seed of love in our hearts,
I ask you to be with me in this time of rest.
Open my heart to receive all you want me to know.
May your Word burst to fulfillment
in the thoughts that I think, the words that I say,
   the deeds that I do.
May I be for you a harvest of righteousness yielding to your will
and empowered by your Word.
To God be all glory and praise, now and forever.

           (Rebecca Bradburn Langer, 1995)

Read and Reflect

[3]I thank my God every time I remember you, [4]constantly praying with joy in every one of my prayers for all of you, [5]because of your sharing in the gospel from the first day until now. [6]I am confident of this, that the one who began a good work among you will bring it to completion by the day of Jesus Christ. [7]It is right for me to think this way about all of you, because you hold me in your heart, for all of you share in God's grace with me, both in my imprisonment and in the defense and confirmation of the gospel. [8]For God is my witness, how I long for all of you with the compassion of Christ Jesus. [9]And this is my prayer, that your love may overflow more and more with knowledge and full insight [10]to help you to determine what is best, so that in the day of Christ you may be pure and blameless, [11]having produced the harvest of righteousness that comes through Jesus Christ for the glory and praise of God. *(Philippians 1:3–11)*

REFLECT

What word or phrase "speaks" to you in this passage? Record here:

Is "confident" a word you use to describe God's good work in your life? If not, what keeps you from this confidence? Name this good work, and live today confident that God is at work in you.

PRAY

RESPOND

To what response is God calling you?

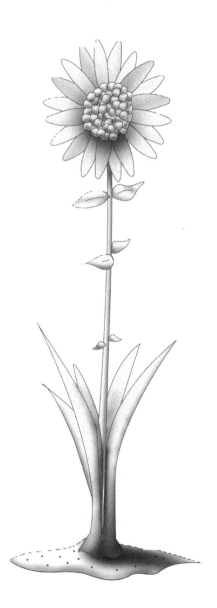

Day Three

REST

God who plants the seed of love in our hearts,
I ask you to be with me in this time of rest.
Open my heart to receive all you want me to know.
May your Word burst to fulfillment
in the thoughts that I think, the words that I say,
    the deeds that I do.
May I be for you a harvest of righteousness yielding to your will
and empowered by your Word.
To God be all glory and praise, now and forever.

(Rebecca Bradburn Langer, 1995)

READ AND REFLECT

[3]I thank my God every time I remember you, [4]constantly praying with joy in every one of my prayers for all of you, [5]because of your sharing in the gospel from the first day until now. [6]I am confident of this, that the one who began a good work among you will bring it to completion by the day of Jesus Christ. [7]It is right for me to think this way about all of you, because you hold me in your heart, for all of you share in God's grace with me, both in my imprisonment and in the defense and confirmation of the gospel. [8]For God is my witness, how I long for all of you with the compassion of Christ Jesus. [9]And this is my prayer, that your love may overflow more and more with knowledge and full insight [10]to help you to determine what is best, so that in the day of Christ you may be pure and blameless, [11]having produced the harvest of righteousness that comes through Jesus Christ for the glory and praise of God. *(Philippians 1:3–11)*

REFLECT

What word or phrase "speaks" to you in this passage? Record here:

Who do you hold in your heart? Picture that person's face and with your hands draw that person into your heart. Hold him or her there as long as you wish—then with an outward motion, offer that person up to God. Repeat with as many people as you wish, and include a person with whom you need a better relationship.

PRAY

RESPOND

To what response is God calling you?

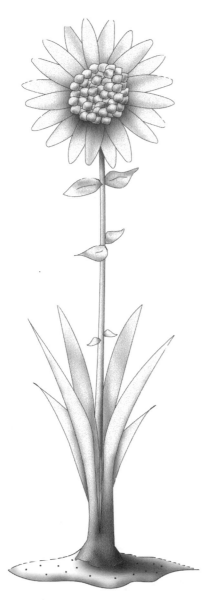

Day Four

Rest

God who plants the seed of love in our hearts,
I ask you to be with me in this time of rest.
Open my heart to receive all you want me to know.
May your Word burst to fulfillment
in the thoughts that I think, the words that I say,
    the deeds that I do.
May I be for you a harvest of righteousness yielding to your will
and empowered by your Word.
To God be all glory and praise, now and forever.

(Rebecca Bradburn Langer, 1995)

Read and Reflect

³I thank my God every time I remember you, ⁴constantly praying with joy in every one of my prayers for all of you, ⁵because of your sharing in the gospel from the first day until now. ⁶I am confident of this, that the one who began a good work among you will bring it to completion by the day of Jesus Christ. ⁷It is right for me to think this way about all of you, because you hold me in your heart, for all of you share in God's grace with me, both in my imprisonment and in the defense and confirmation of the gospel. ⁸For God is my witness, how I long for all of you with the compassion of Christ Jesus. ⁹And this is my prayer, that your love may overflow more and more with knowledge and full insight ¹⁰to help you to determine what is best, so that in the day of Christ you may be pure and blameless, ¹¹having produced the harvest of righteousness that comes through Jesus Christ for the glory and praise of God. *(Philippians 1:3–11)*

REFLECT

What word or phrase "speaks" to you in this passage? Record here:

As you participate in this weekly study, how are the disciplines helping you have "more knowledge and insight" into God's will for you? Make a symbol for how God is working in you (or write a poem or parable that expresses this). Share this with someone you feel led to share it with today.

PRAY

RESPOND

To what response is God calling you?

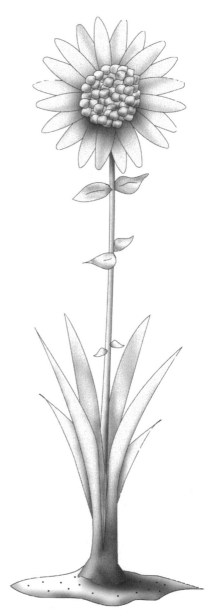

Day Five

REST

God who plants the seed of love in our hearts,
I ask you to be with me in this time of rest.
Open my heart to receive all you want me to know.
May your Word burst to fulfillment
in the thoughts that I think, the words that I say,
    the deeds that I do.
May I be for you a harvest of righteousness yielding to your will
and empowered by your Word.
To God be all glory and praise, now and forever.

(Rebecca Bradburn Langer, 1995)

READ AND REFLECT

[3]I thank my God every time I remember you, [4]constantly praying with joy in every one of my prayers for all of you, [5]because of your sharing in the gospel from the first day until now. [6]I am confident of this, that the one who began a good work among you will bring it to completion by the day of Jesus Christ. [7]It is right for me to think this way about all of you, because you hold me in your heart, for all of you share in God's grace with me, both in my imprisonment and in the defense and confirmation of the gospel. [8]For God is my witness, how I long for all of you with the compassion of Christ Jesus. [9]And this is my prayer, that your love may overflow more and more with knowledge and full insight [10]to help you to determine what is best, so that in the day of Christ you may be pure and blameless, [11]having produced the harvest of righteousness that comes through Jesus Christ for the glory and praise of God. (*Philippians 1:3–11*)

REFLECT

What word or phrase "speaks" to you in this passage? Record here:

Let this word or phrase be a refrain (or a mantra) for you today. Repeat it several times throughout the day as a way of remembering God's presence with you and a reminder that you are growing into a harvest of righteousness. You may also want to write it a number of times on a small sheet of paper and place it where you can see it today.

PRAY

RESPOND

To what response is God calling you?

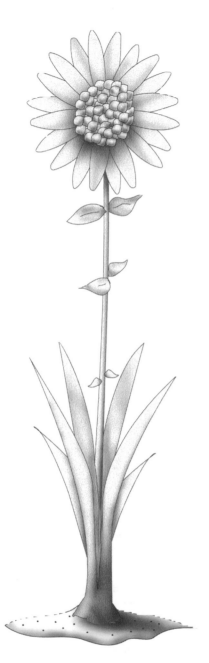

Day Six

Rest

God who plants the seed of love in our hearts,
I ask you to be with me in this time of rest.
Open my heart to receive all you want me to know.
May your Word burst to fulfillment
in the thoughts that I think, the words that I say,
    the deeds that I do.
May I be for you a harvest of righteousness yielding to your will
and empowered by your Word.
To God be all glory and praise, now and forever.

(Rebecca Bradburn Langer, 1995)

Read and Reflect

[3]I thank my God every time I remember you, [4]constantly praying with joy in every one of my prayers for all of you, [5]because of your sharing in the gospel from the first day until now. [6]I am confident of this, that the one who began a good work among you will bring it to completion by the day of Jesus Christ. [7]It is right for me to think this way about all of you, because you hold me in your heart, for all of you share in God's grace with me, both in my imprisonment and in the defense and confirmation of the gospel. [8]For God is my witness, how I long for all of you with the compassion of Christ Jesus. [9]And this is my prayer, that your love may overflow more and more with knowledge and full insight [10]to help you to determine what is best, so that in the day of Christ you may be pure and blameless, [11]having produced the harvest of righteousness that comes through Jesus Christ for the glory and praise of God. (Philippians 1:3–11)

REFLECT

What word or phrase "speaks" to you in this passage? Record here:

All our lives, we are in the process of producing a harvest of what is right and good for God. Choose one thing that you have realized is part of your offering to God from the weeks spent in this study. Choose a way to show this, such as a movement, a piece of art, a color, a shape, a song, or another form of expression.

PRAY

RESPOND

To what response is God calling you?

Group Meeting Day

Rest

The leader begins by inviting the group to rest in this prayer, making it into a group prayer by changing "I," "me," and "my" to "we," "us," and "our."

> God who plants the seed of love in our hearts,
> We ask you to be with us in this time of rest.
> Open our hearts to receive all you want us to know.
> May your Word burst to fulfillment
> in the thoughts that we think, the words that we say,
>   the deeds that we do.
> May we be for you a harvest of righteousness yielding to your will
> and empowered by your Word.
> To God be all glory and praise, now and forever.
>
> (Rebecca Bradburn Langer, 1995)

Read and Reflect

The group leader reads the scripture aloud, followed by silence.

[3]I thank my God every time I remember you, [4]constantly praying with joy in every one of my prayers for all of you, [5]because of your sharing in the gospel from the first day until now. [6]I am confident of this, that the one who began a good work among you will bring it to completion by the day of Jesus Christ. [7]It is right for me to think this way about all of you, because you hold me in your heart, for all of you share in God's grace with me, both in my imprisonment and in the defense and confirmation of the gospel. [8]For God is my witness, how I long for all of you with the compassion

of Christ Jesus. ⁹And this is my prayer, that your love may overflow more and more with knowledge and full insight ¹⁰to help you to determine what is best, so that in the day of Christ you may be pure and blameless, ¹¹having produced the harvest of righteousness that comes through Jesus Christ for the glory and praise of God.

(Philippians 1:3–11)

REFLECT

The leader has group members record the word or phrase that "spoke" to them. Then they can share that word or phrase or another one that resonated with them during the past week. Each person shares one "seed" to take from this study to strengthen his or her "harvest of righteousness."

PRAY

Have a time after each person has shared to pray for each individual and his or her continued growth in God.

RESPOND

To what response is God calling you? Because this is the last week, the group may want to make a new covenant to meet for another four weeks, using the devotional reading method in one of the gospels. If this will be the last time you meet as a group, thank God for the time spent together. Close using a piece that the group chooses from the workbook or something by one of the group members.

Additional Reflection Selections

[1]I am the true vine, and [*God*] my Father [*and Mother*] is the vinedresser. [2]Every branch of mine that bears no fruit, God takes away, and every branch that does bear fruit God prunes, that it may bear more fruit. [3]You are already made clean by the word which I have spoken to you. [4]Abide in me, and I in you. As the branch cannot bear fruit by itself, unless it abides in the vine, neither can you, unless you abide in me. [5]I am the vine, you are the branches. All who abide in me, and I in them, they are the ones who bear much fruit, for apart from me you can do nothing. [6]Any one who does not abide in me is cast forth as a branch and withers; and the branches are gathered, thrown into the fire and burned. [7]If you abide in me, and my words abide in you, ask whatever you will, and it shall be done for you. [8]By this God is glorified, that you bear much fruit, and so prove to be my disciples. [9]As [*God*] the Father [*and Mother*] has loved me, so have I loved you; abide in my love. [10]If you keep my commandments, you will abide in my love, just as I have kept God's commandments and abide in God's love.[11]These things I have spoken to you, that my joy may be in you, and that your joy may be full. [12]This is my commandment, that you love one another as I have loved you. [13]Greater love has no one than this, that one lay down one's life for a friend. [14]You are my friends if you do what I command you. [15]No longer do I call you servants, for the servant does not know what the master is doing; but I have called you friends, for all that I have heard from God I have made known to you. [16]You did not choose me, but I chose you and appointed you that you should go and bear fruit and that your fruit should abide; so that whatever you ask [*God*] the Father [*and Mother*] in my name may be given to you. [17]This I command you, to love one another. (John 15:1–17, from *An Inclusive-Language Lectionary*, Year B)

Typically people ask, Are there any clues to whether or not I am growing spiritually? Paul suggests there is one test, namely, growth in the fruit of the Spirit: "The fruit of the Spirit is love, joy, peace, patience, kindness, generosity, faithfulness, gentleness, and self-control" (Galatians 5:22–23). So often people describe a single fruit comprised of numerous characteristics. Our spiritual life is improving when all of these dimensions of a single fruit are present.... (From *Spiritual Life: The Foundation for Preaching and Teaching*, Westerhoff, 1994, pp. 8–9)

From Mechtild of Magdeburg:
From the very beginning, God loved us.
The Holy Trinity gave itself in the creation of all things,
and made us, body and soul, in infinite love.
We were fashioned most nobly. God takes such delight in the human person
that Divinity sings this song to our souls:
O love rose on the thorn!
O hovering bee in the honey!
O pure dove in your being!
O glorious sun in your setting!
O full moon in your course!
From you, I your God, will never turn away.

Jesus, Remember Me

Jesus, remember me
when You come into Your kingdom.
Jesus, remember me
when You come into Your kingdom.

(*Presbyterian Hymnal*, no. 599)

Love is a fruit in season at all times.
Mother Teresa

As Those of Old Their Firstfruits Brought

As those of old their firstfruits brought Of vineyard, flock, and
field
To God, the giver of all good, The source of bounteous yield.
So we today our firstfruits bring, The wealth of this good land:
Of farm and market, shop and home, Of mind and heart and
hand.

A world in need now summons us To labor, love, and give,
To make our life an offering To God that all may live.
The church of Christ is calling us To make the dream come true:
A world redeemed by Christ-like love, All life in Christ made new.

With gratitude and humble trust We bring our best to You,
Not just to serve Your cause, but share Your love with neighbors
too.
O God who gave Yourself to us In Jesus Christ Your Son,
Help us to give ourselves each day Until life's work is done.

Frank von Christierson, 1960 (*Presbyterian Hymnal*, no. 414)

Gloria, Gloria

Gloria, gloria, in excelsis Deo!
Gloria, gloria, alleluia, alleluia!

(*Presbyterian Hymnal*, no. 576)

My flesh and my heart may fail,
  but God is the strength of my heart and my portion forever.
(Psalm 73:26)

John Calvin on prayer:
  …that our hearts may be aroused and borne to God,
  whether to praise him or to beseech his help—from this we
  may understand that the essentials of prayer are set in the
  mind and heart, or rather that prayer itself is properly an
  emotion of the heart within, which is poured out and laid
  open before God, the searcher of hearts. (Calvin 1960, 891;
  cf. Rom. 8:27, III.xx.28)

Words fail to explain how necessary prayer is, and in how many ways the exercise of prayer is profitable. (Calvin 1960, 851, III.xx.2)

John Calvin on scripture:

Christ cannot be known anywhere but the scriptures . . . it follows that the scriptures should be read with the aim of finding Christ in them. (Calvin 1960, 139, *Commentary on John* 5:39, CC4/139)

On the Genevan Catechism (1545):

The Cathechism speaks of the fruits or benefits of scripture: "(scripture) . . . once engraved on our hearts and its roots fixed there, so that it will bring forth fruit in our life; if finally we be formed to its rule, then it will turn to our salvation." (Adams, 4)

RECORD YOUR OWN THOUGHTS AND REFLECTIONS HERE:

Works Cited

Adams, Richard D. "The Whole Counsel of God." Unpublished paper.

Baxter, Richard. 1847. *Saint's Everlasting Rest*. Philadelphia: Presbyterian Board of Publication.

Calvin, John. 1960. *Institutes of Christian Religion*. Edited by John T. McNeill and translated by Ford Lewis Battles. Philadelphia: The Westminster Press.

Conder, Josiah. *The Presbyterian Hymnal* (501). 1990. Louisville, Ky.: Westminster/John Knox Press.

De Sola, Carla. 1991. *The Spirit Moves: A Handbook of Dance and Prayer*. Richmond, Calif.

Doddridge, Philip. n.d. *Religion in the Soul*. Reprint, Philadelphia: Presbyterian Board of Publication.

Doyle, Brendan. 1983. *Meditations with Julian of Norwich*. Santa Fe, N.M.: Bear & Company.

Eckhart, Meister. 1986. *Meister Eckhart, Teacher and Preacher*. The Classics of Western Spirituality, Paulist Press.

Edwards, Jonathan. 1972. *The Great Awakening*, ed. C. C. Goen, New Haven, Yale University Press.

Hinton, Jeanne. 1995. *A Year of Prayer*. Minneapolis: Augsburg Fortress.

An Inclusive-Language Lectionary: Readings for Year B. 1987. Revised Edition. Division of Education and Ministry, National Council of the Churches of Christ in the U.S.A. Atlanta: John Knox Press; New York: The Pilgrim Press; and Philadelphia: The Westminster Press.

Nouwen, Henri J. 1995. *With Open Hands*. Notre Dame, Ind.: Ave Maria Press.

Office of the General Assembly. 1996. *Book of Confessions*. Louisville, Ky.: Office of the General Assembly of the Presbyterian Church (U.S.A.).

Office of the General Assembly. 1996. *Book of Order*. Louisville, Ky.: Office of the General Assembly of the Presbyterian Church (U.S.A).

The Presbyterian Hymnal. 1990. Louisville, Ky.: Westminster/John Knox Press.

Rice, Howard. 1991. *Reformed Spirituality*. Louisville, Ky.: Westminster/John Knox Press.

Thompson, Marjorie J. 1995. *Soul Feast*. Louisville, Ky.: Westminster/John Knox Press.

Thurman, Anne. 1991. *For the Inward Journey: The Writings of Howard Thurman*. Richmond, Ind.: Friends United Press.

Thurman, Howard. 1972. *Deep Is the Hunger*. Richmond, Ind.: Friends United Press.

Thurman, Howard. 1976. *Meditations of the Heart*.

Uhlein, Gabriele. 1982. *Meditations with Hildegard of Bingen*. Sante Fe, N.M.: Bear & Company.

von Balthasar, Hans Urs. 1955. *Prayer*. San Francisco: Ignatius Press.

Westerhoff, John. 1994. *The Spiritual Life: The Foundation for Preaching and Teaching*. Louisville, Ky.: Westminster/John Knox Press.

Woodruff, Sue. 1982. *Meditations with Mechthild of Magdeburg*. Santa Fe, N.M.: Bear & Company.

Music and Other Resources

Dreitcer, Andy, and Joy Luscombe. "Water Our Lives" Used with permission. To request for use write: 2 Kensington Road, San Anselmo, California 94960.

Taize Music Tapes can be obtained from most Christian Bookstores or from G.I.A. Publications, Inc., 7404 South Mason Ave., Chicago, Illinois 60638.

Bear & Co. Publishing, 506 Aqua Fria Street, Santa Fe, New Mexico 87501.